a Shelter for Sadness

ANNE BOOTH & DAVID LITCHFIELD

templar
books

Sadness has come to live with me
and I am building it a shelter.

I am building a shelter for my Sadness
and welcoming it inside.

I am giving it a space
for it to sit

or lie down.

To curl up very,
very small,

or be as **big** as it can be.

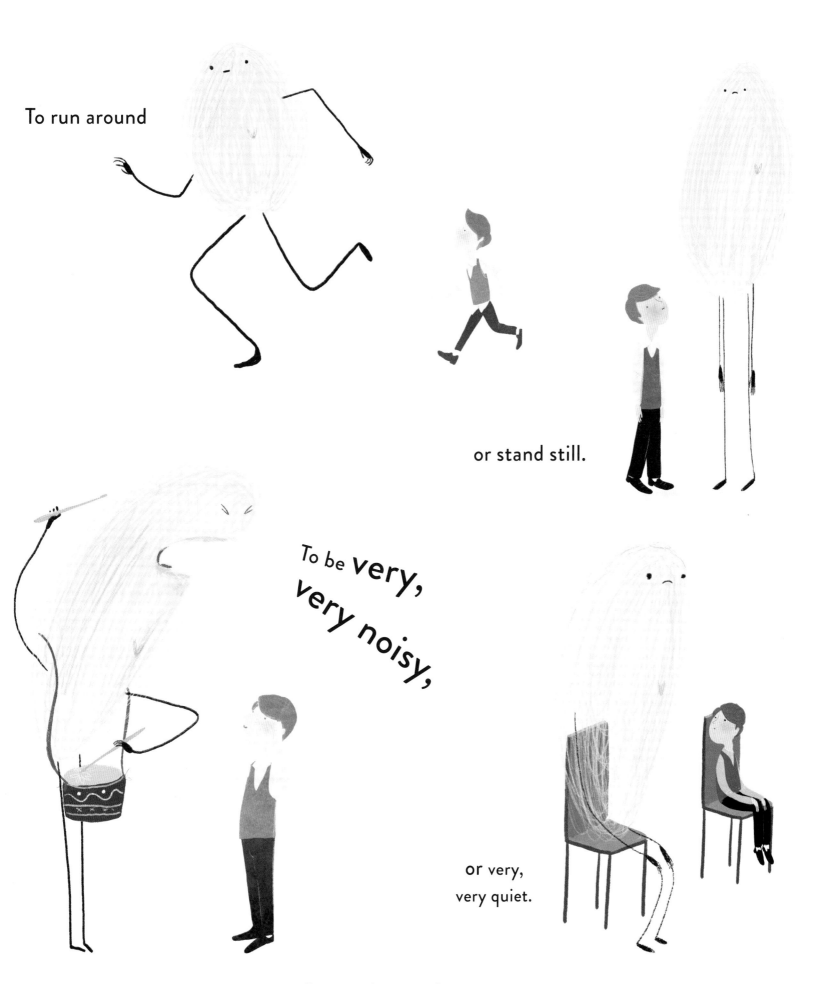

To run around

or stand still.

To be **very, very noisy,**

or very, very quiet.

Or anything in between.

In this shelter for Sadness it can turn to the wall
or look out through the window, in the middle of the night . . .

or in the day.
The windows will open to let sounds in,
or close to keep them out.

The shelter I will build
for my Sadness
will have light from the sun
or from the moon and stars.

But the windows will have curtains
that Sadness can draw when it wants to.
And there will be candles or lamps
if Sadness needs them.

Lots and lots of light . . .

or no light at all.

Sadness can sit in darkness if it wants to.

Whatever it feels like.

Because this is the shelter for my Sadness,
and it has a right to be there.
And I will make my shelter strong, so that in winter
Sadness will have a safe shelter against the storms.

But I will give it a little garden too,
so that in spring, birds will come and build their nests
and green shoots will peek through the dark earth.

In summer, roses will bloom,
and their scent will steal in under the door.
And my Sadness can open the windows
and breathe in and smell them.

If it wants to.

In autumn it can look out at the trees,
and cry when the leaves turn red and orange
and fall to the ground.

Or it can go out and walk through the leaves
and hear the sounds they make.

It can build bonfires and dance around them,

or sit quietly and watch the flames.

Anything it needs to.

Sometimes I will visit my Sadness

in its shelter every day.

Every hour if needed.

Sometimes we will run

into each other's arms and hug and cry,

and talk . . .

and sometimes just sit next to each other

saying nothing.

Sometimes I will be too busy to visit Sadness for a while.

But that is okay too.

I have built a good shelter for my Sadness

and it is safe inside, and nobody will hurt it.

I can visit it whenever I need to.
Whenever it calls to me.

And, whenever Sadness wants,
it can come out of its shelter
and hold my hand.

And we will look out at the world
and discover how beautiful it is.
Together.